GEOMETRY WORKBOOK FOR 2ND GRADE

Math Workbooks Children's Geometry Books

Speedy Publishing LLC

40 E. Main St. #1156

Newark, DE 19711

www.speedypublishing.com

Copyright 2018

DRAW A LINE TO MATCH THE SHAPES AND THEIR NAMES!

   •   •   HEXAGON

   •   •   CIRCLE

   •   •   SQUARE

   •   •   TRIANGLE

EXERCISE NO. 2

PENTAGON

RECTANGLE

STAR

DIAMOND

OVAL

TRAPEZIUM

OCTAGON

HEART

EXERCISE NO. 4

•   • POLYGON

•   • URVILINEAR TRIANGLE

•   • QUATREFOIL

•   • ARROW

EXERCISE NO. 5

• PARALLELOGRAM

• HEPTAGON

• CROSS

• CRESCENT

COLOR THE
SHAPES!

EXERCISE NO. 6

- Color the squares

● Color the rectangles

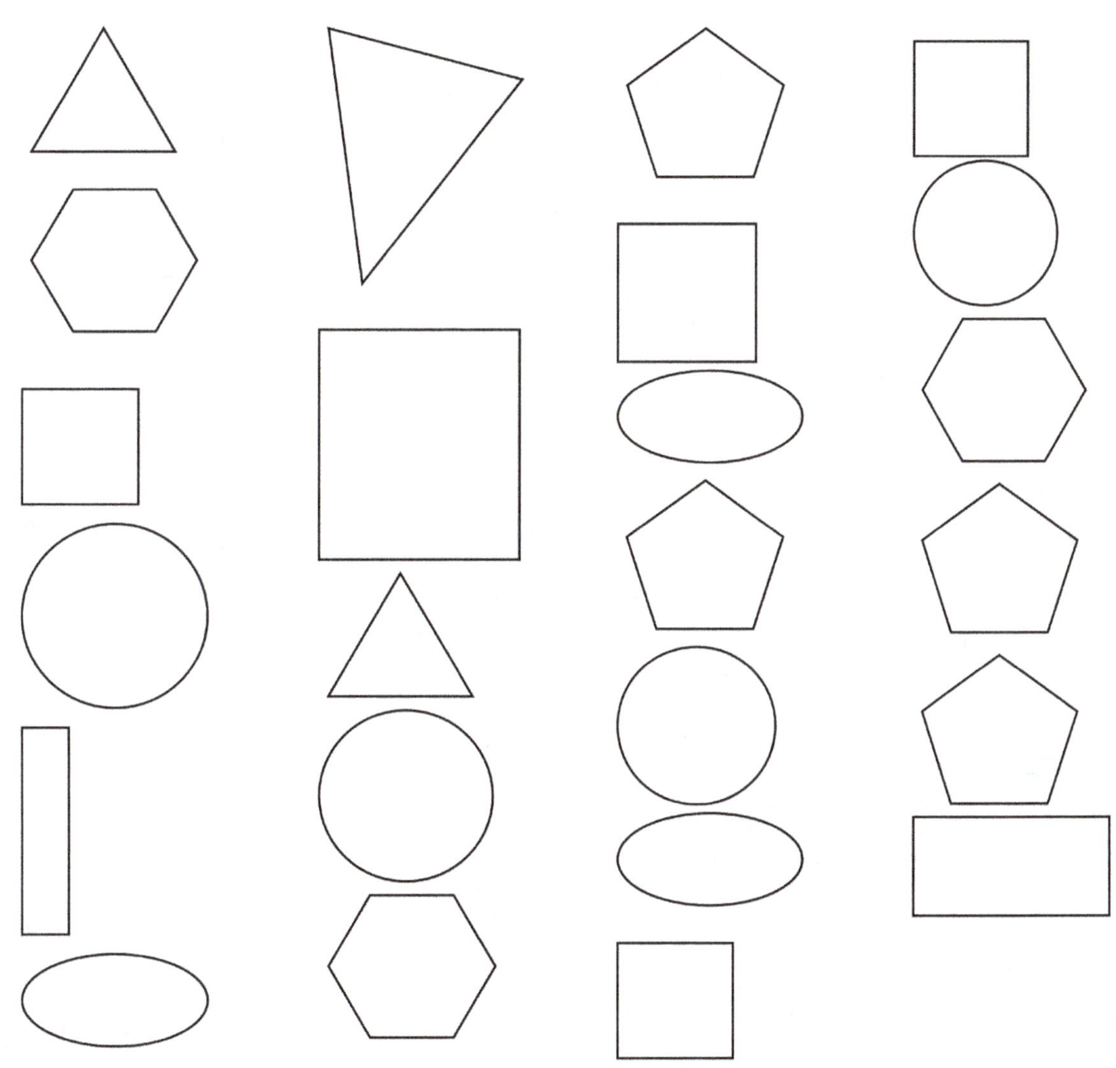

EXERCISE NO. 8

• Color the triangles

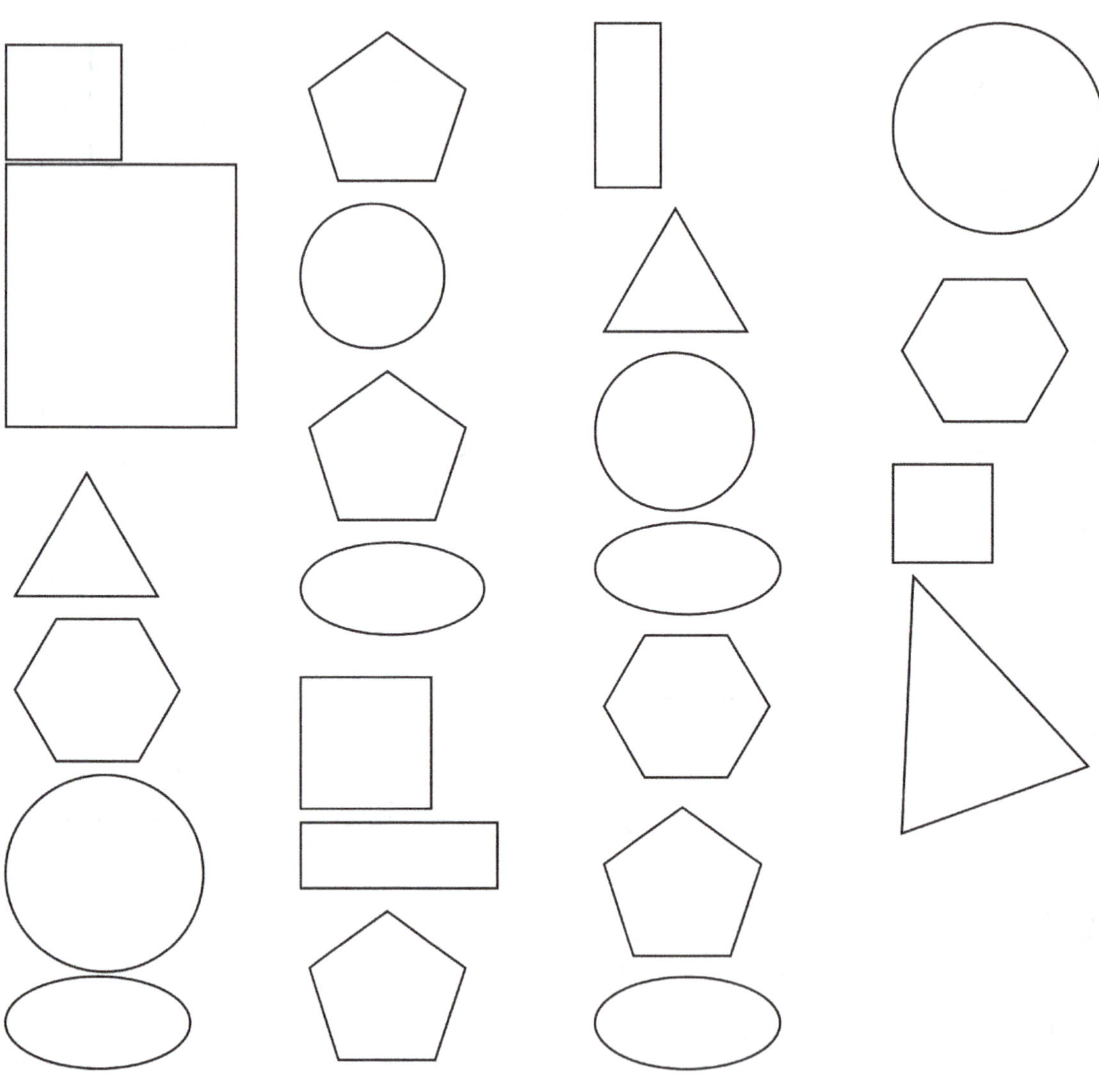

- Color the circles

EXERCISE NO. 10

- Color the ovals

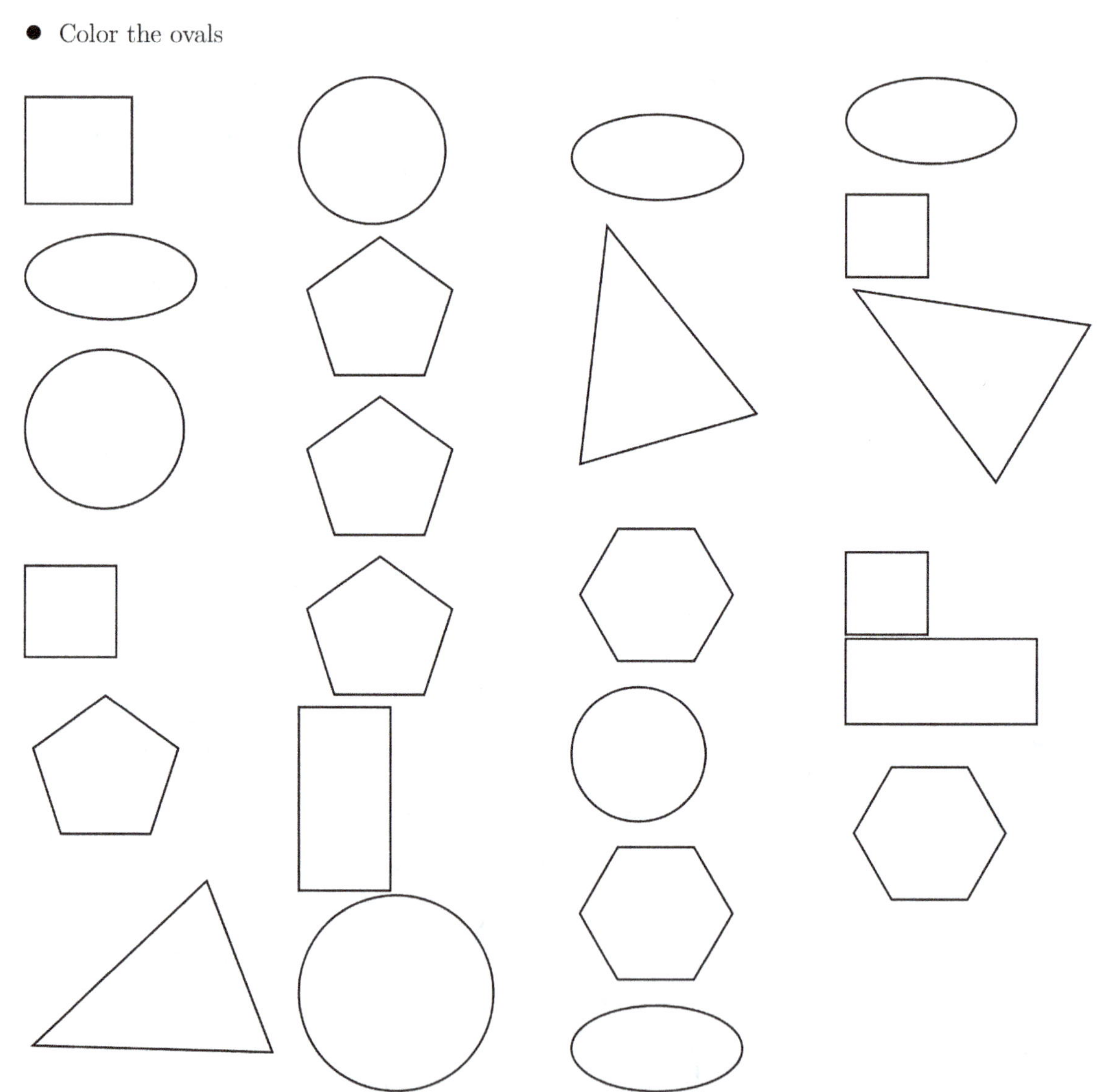

EXERCISE NO. II

- Color the pentagons

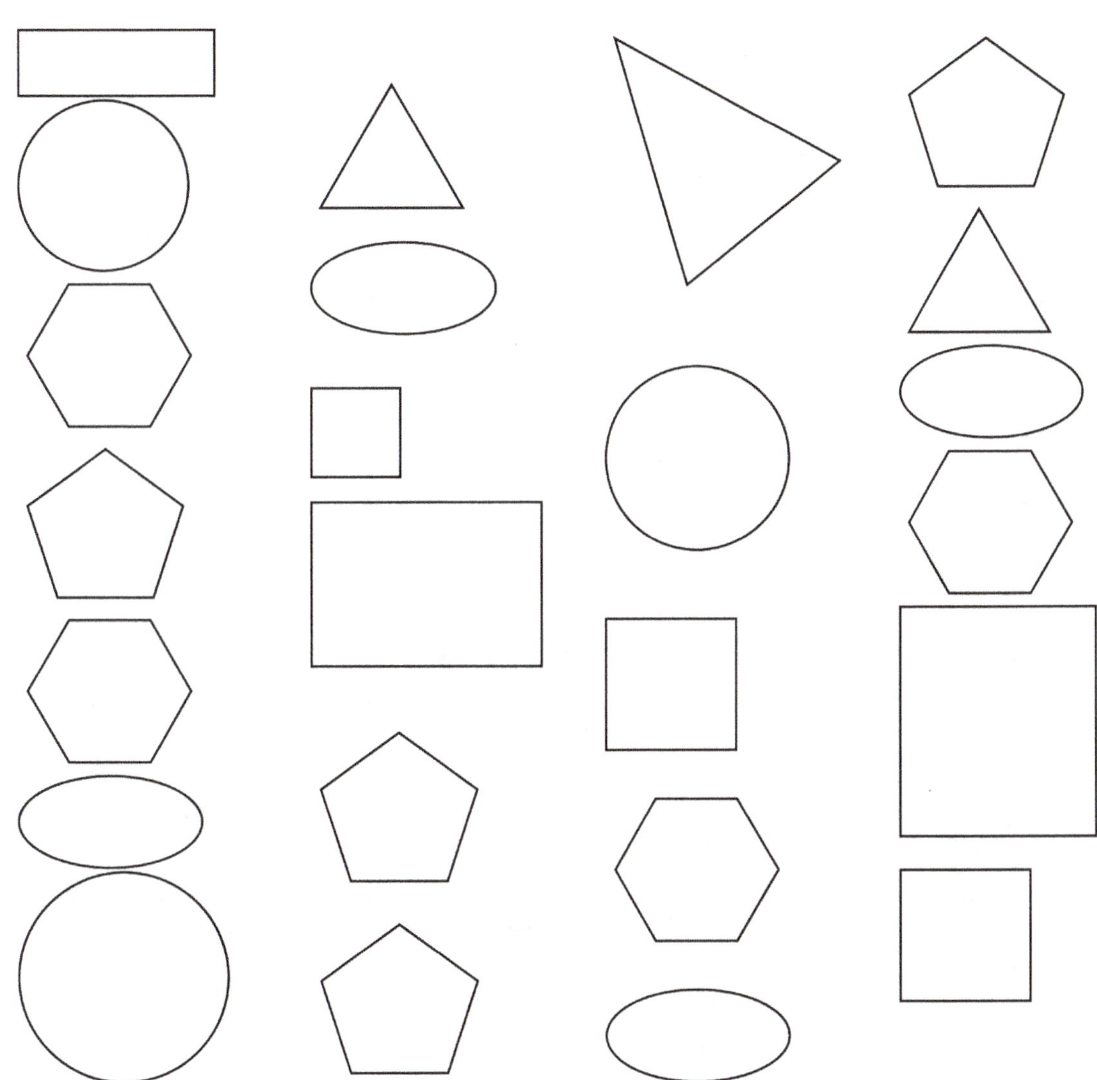

● Color the hexagons

CIRCLE THE ODD
ONE OUT!

 ELLIPSE

 CIRCLE

 CROSS

 PENTAGON

 SQUARE

 PENTAGON

 RECTANGLE

 CROSS

 CIRCLE

 TRIANGLE

 DIAMOND

 SQUARE

 ELLIPSE

FIND THE ONE IMAGE WITHOUT A DUPLICATE

 DIAMOND

 TRIANGLE

HEXAGON

STAR

QUATREFOIL

POLYGON

HEART

HEXAGON

QUATREFOIL

TRAPEZIUM

STAR

PARALLELOGRAM

TRAPEZIUM

POLYGON

PARALLELOGRAM

FIND THE ONE IMAGE WITHOUT A DUPLICATE

OCTAGON

HEART

ARROW
HEPTAGON
CRESCENT
CURVILINEAR TRIANGLE
HEPTAGON
CRESCENT
FIND THE
ONE
IMAGE
WITHOUT A DUPLICATE
?
ARROW
CURVILINEAR TRIANGLE

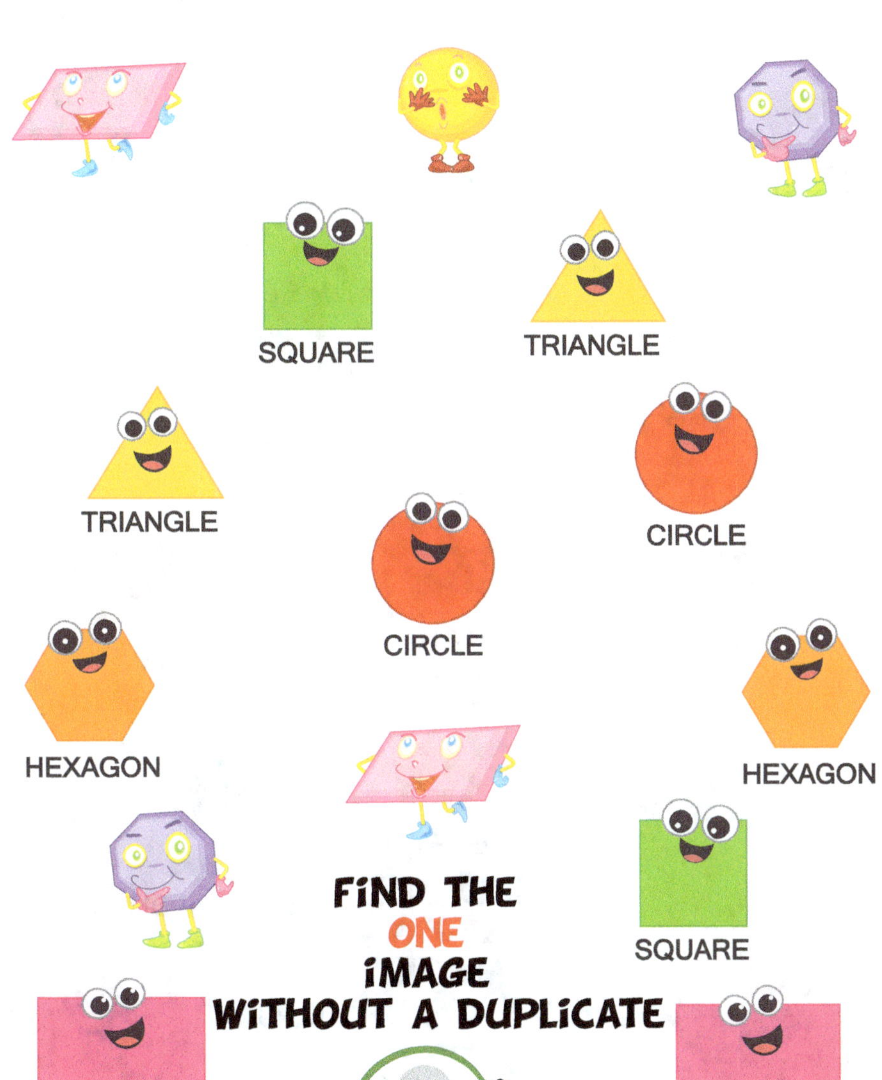

SQUARE
TRIANGLE
TRIANGLE
CIRCLE
CIRCLE
HEXAGON
HEXAGON
SQUARE
FIND THE
ONE
IMAGE
WITHOUT A DUPLICATE
RECTANGLE
RECTANGLE
?

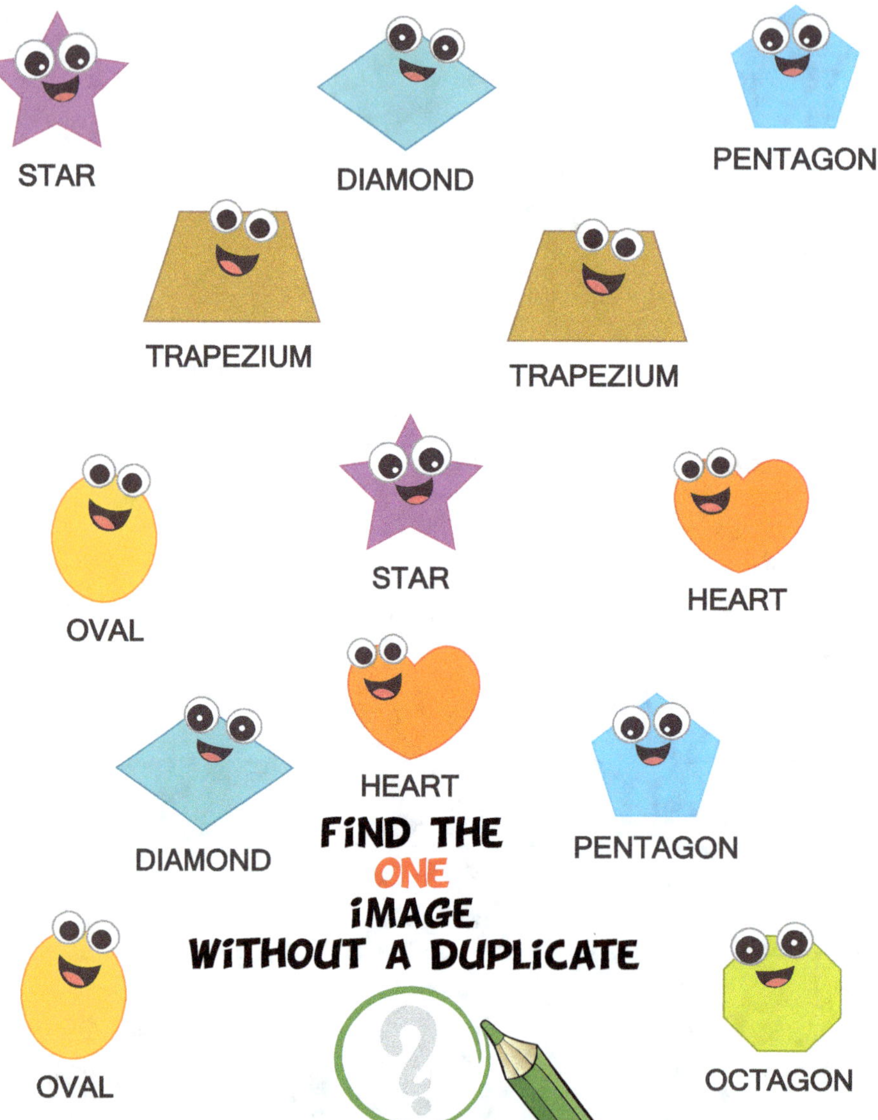
STAR
DIAMOND
PENTAGON
TRAPEZIUM
TRAPEZIUM
OVAL
STAR
HEART
DIAMOND
HEART
PENTAGON
FIND THE
ONE
IMAGE
WITHOUT A DUPLICATE
OVAL
OCTAGON
?

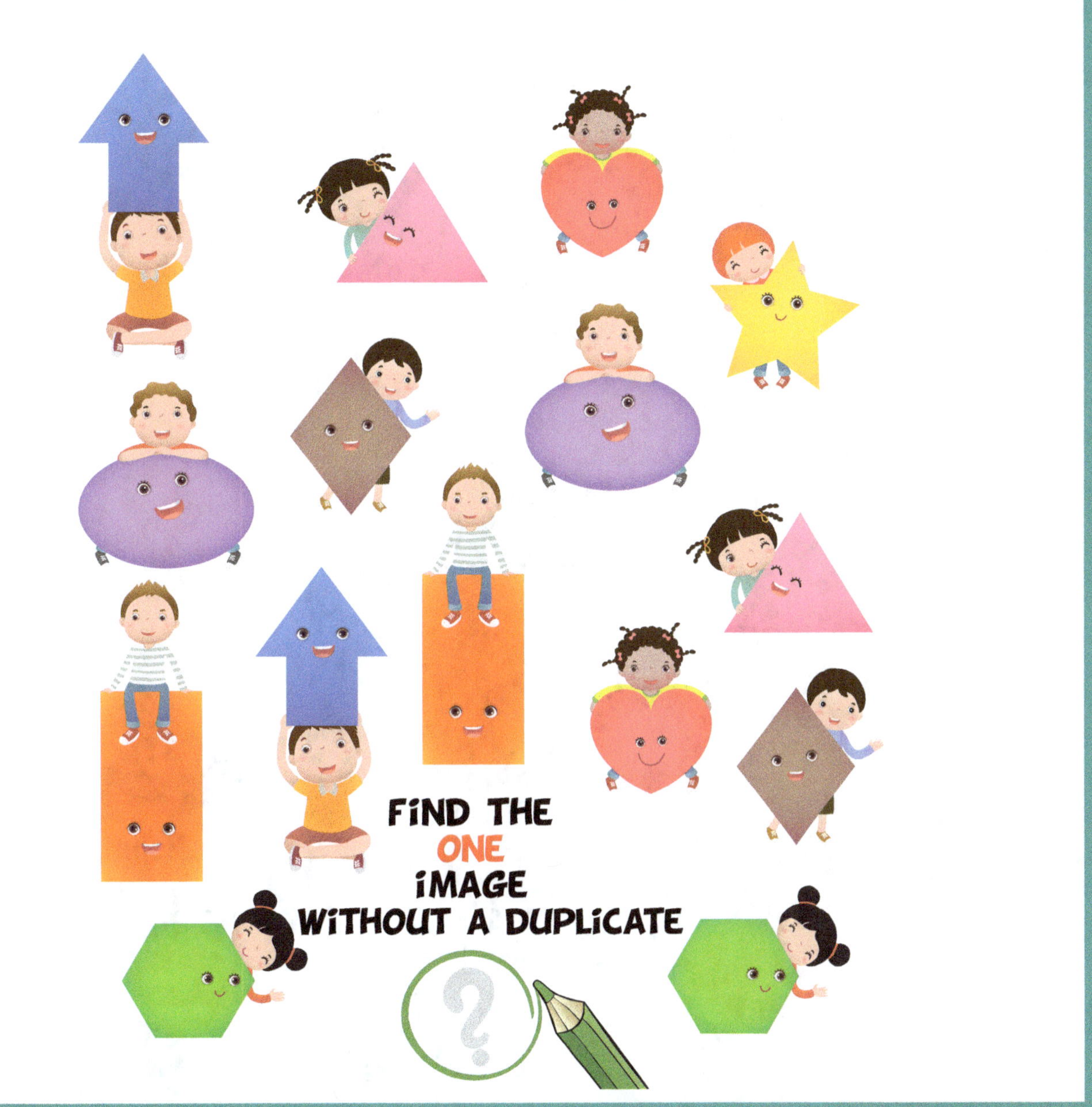
FIND THE
ONE
IMAGE
WITHOUT A DUPLICATE
?

SQUARE

TRIANGLE

RECTANGLE

CIRCLE

STAR

CIRCLE

SQUARE

PENTAGON

TRIANGLE

TRAPEZIUM

DIAMOND

RECTANGLE

DIAMOND

FIND THE ONE IMAGE WITHOUT A DUPLICATE

PENTAGON

TRAPEZIUM

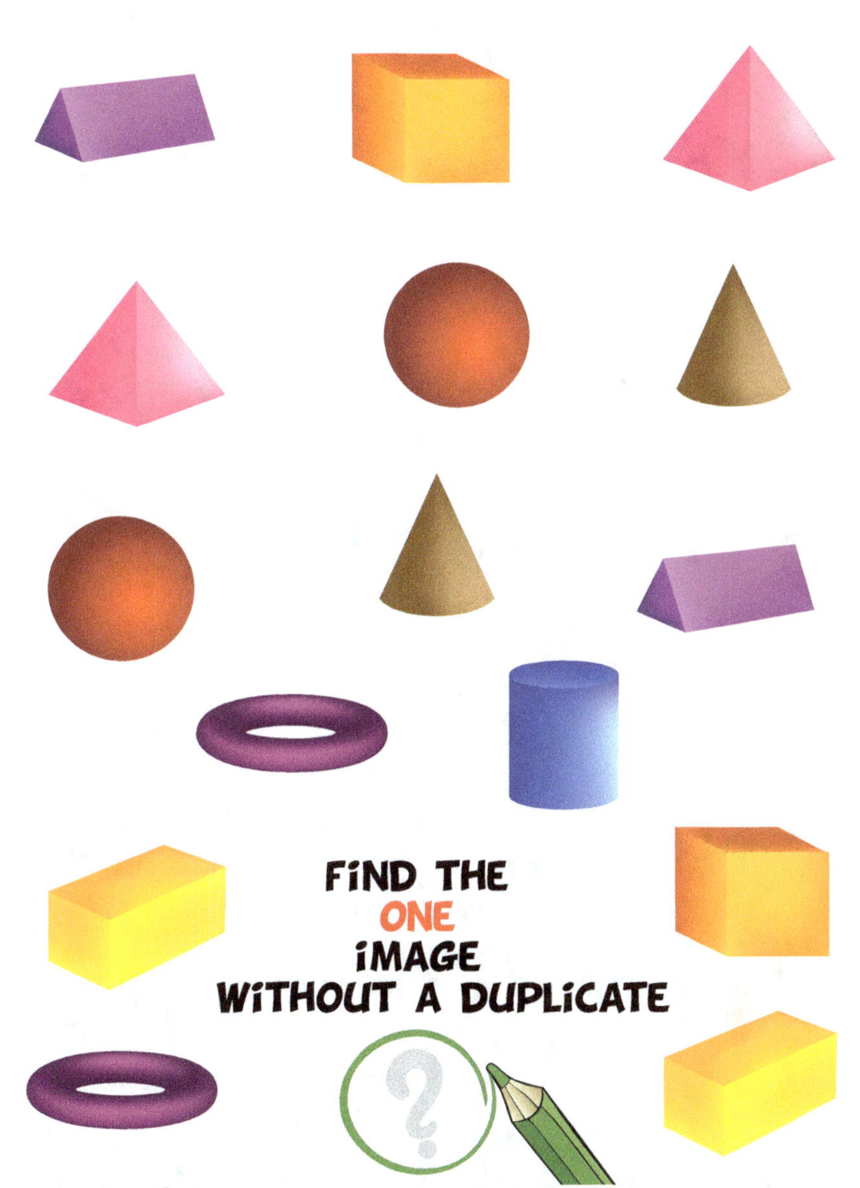
FIND THE
ONE
IMAGE
WITHOUT A DUPLICATE

EXERCISE NO. 21

FIND THE
ONE
IMAGE
WITHOUT A DUPLICATE

MATCHING GAME!

3D SHAPES

EXERCISE NO. 25

EXERCISE NO. 26

EXERCISE NO. 27

EXERCISE NO. 28

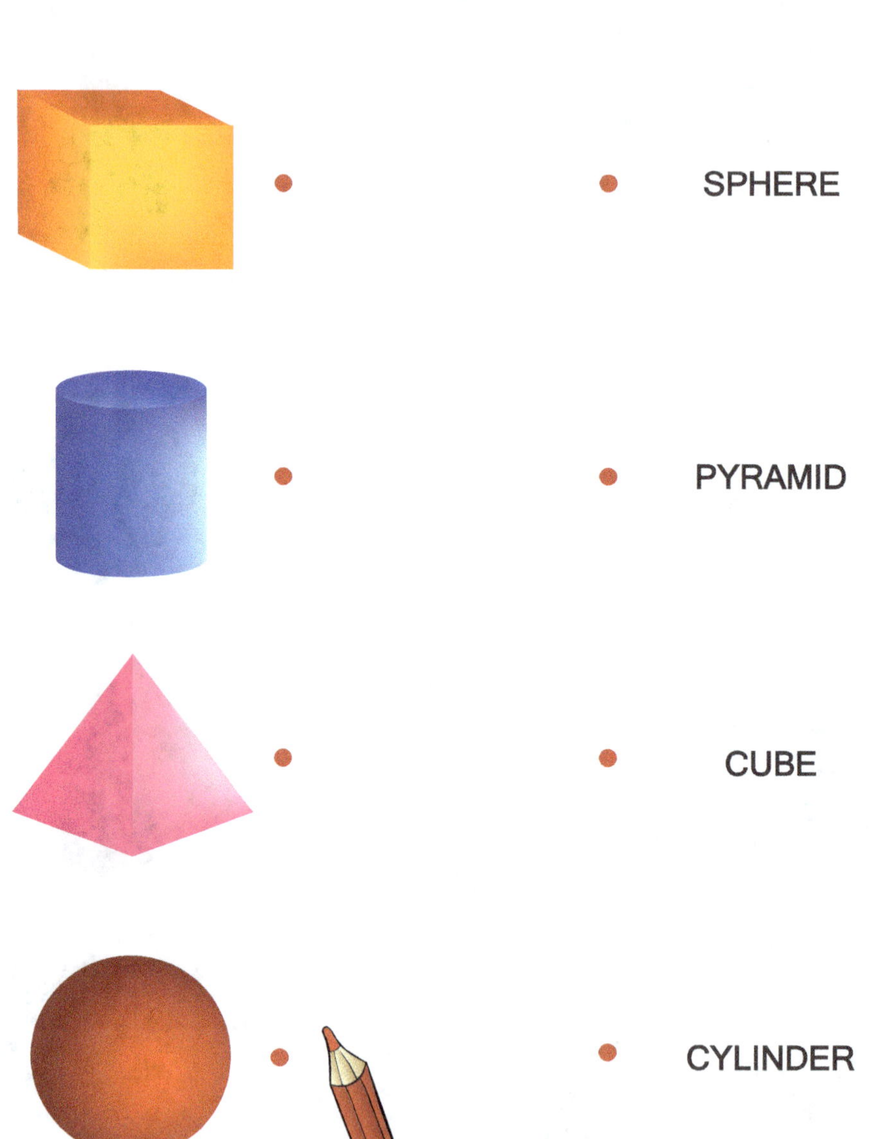

EXERCISE NO. 29

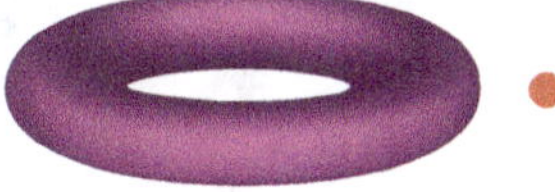

- TORUS
- CONE
- HEMISPHERE
- CUBOID

EXERCISE NO. 30

EXERCISE NO. 31

COLOR THE SHAPE
THAT MATCHES THE
FIGURE ABOVE!

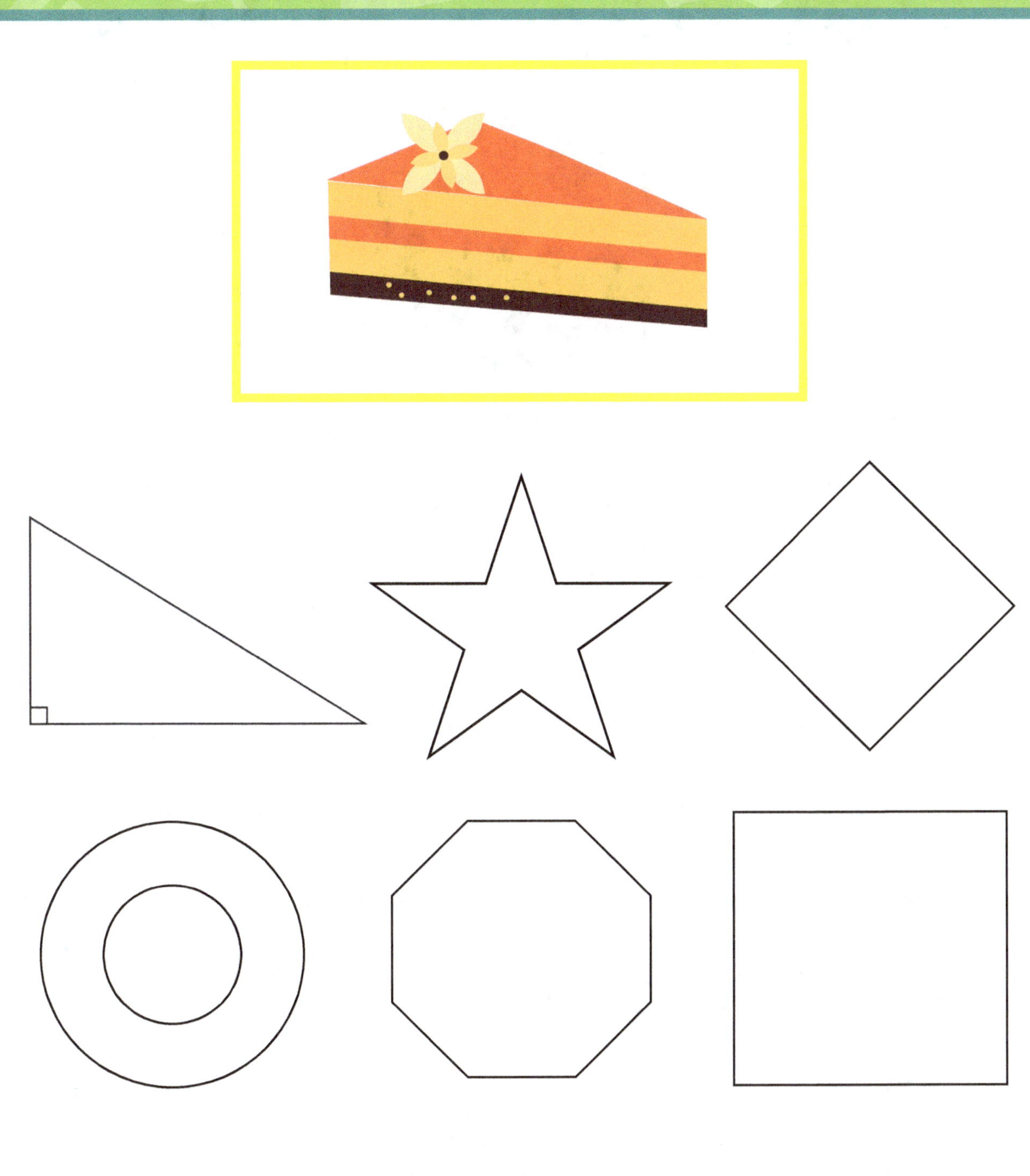

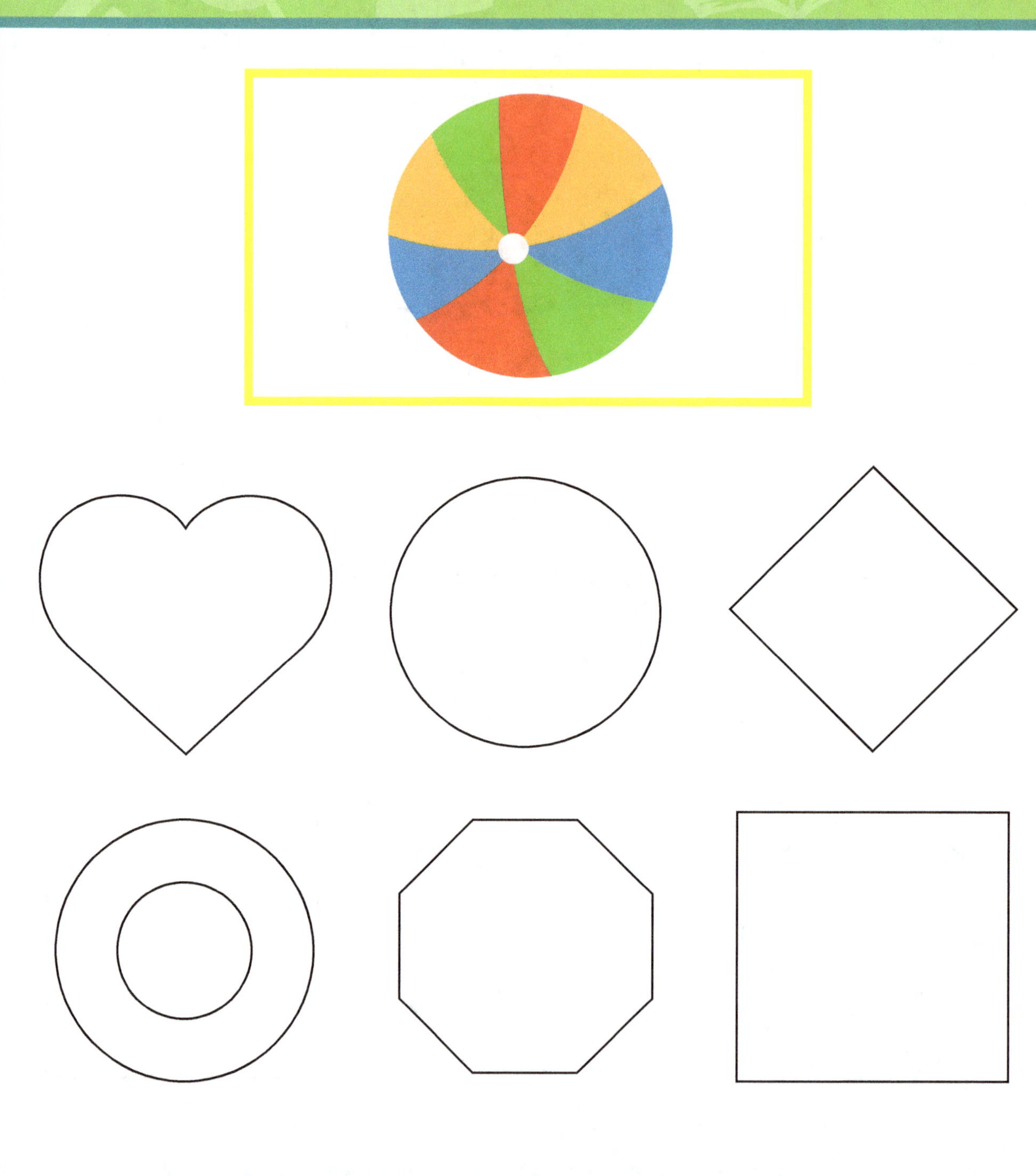

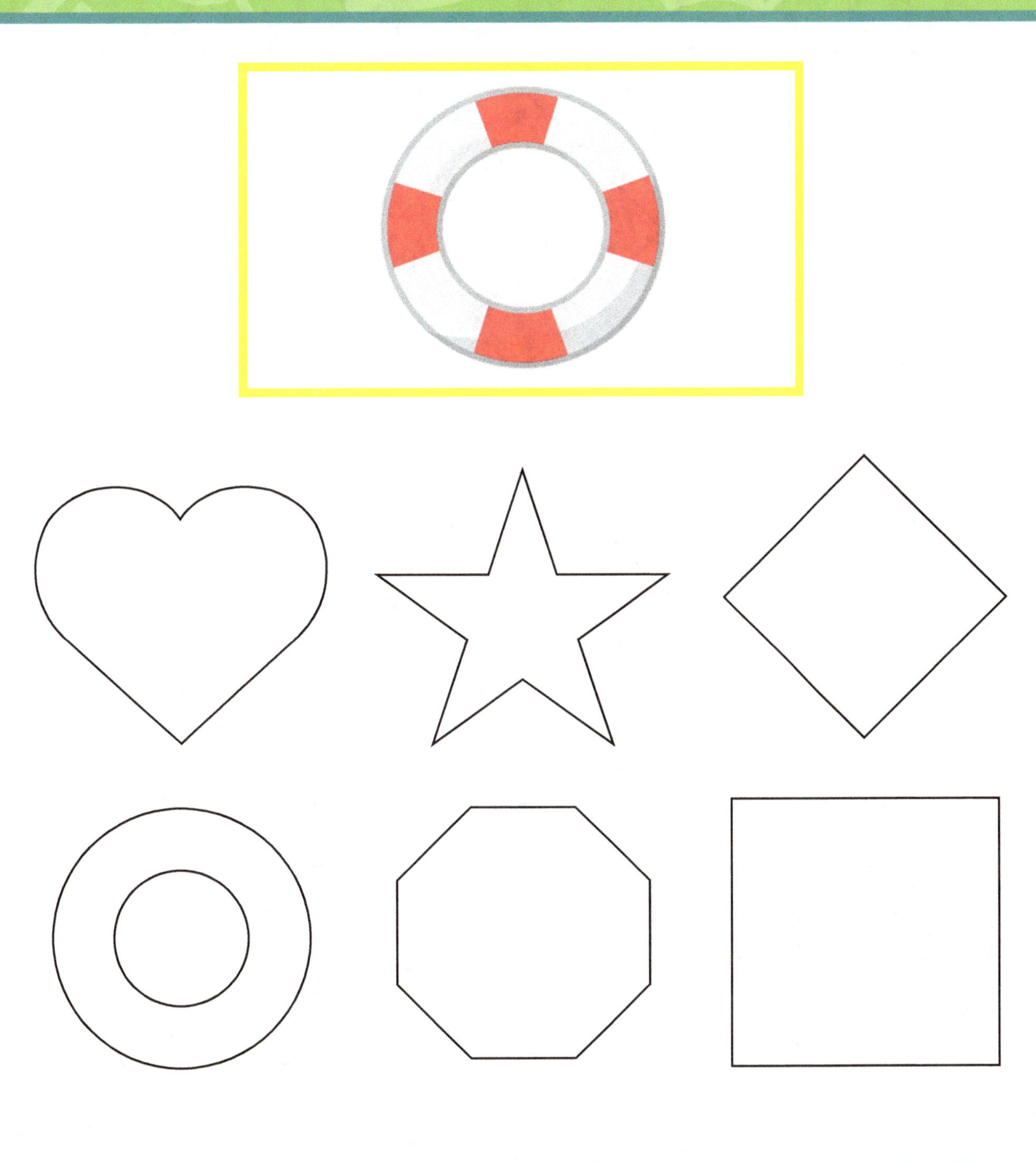

DANGER
CROCODILES
NO
SWIMMING

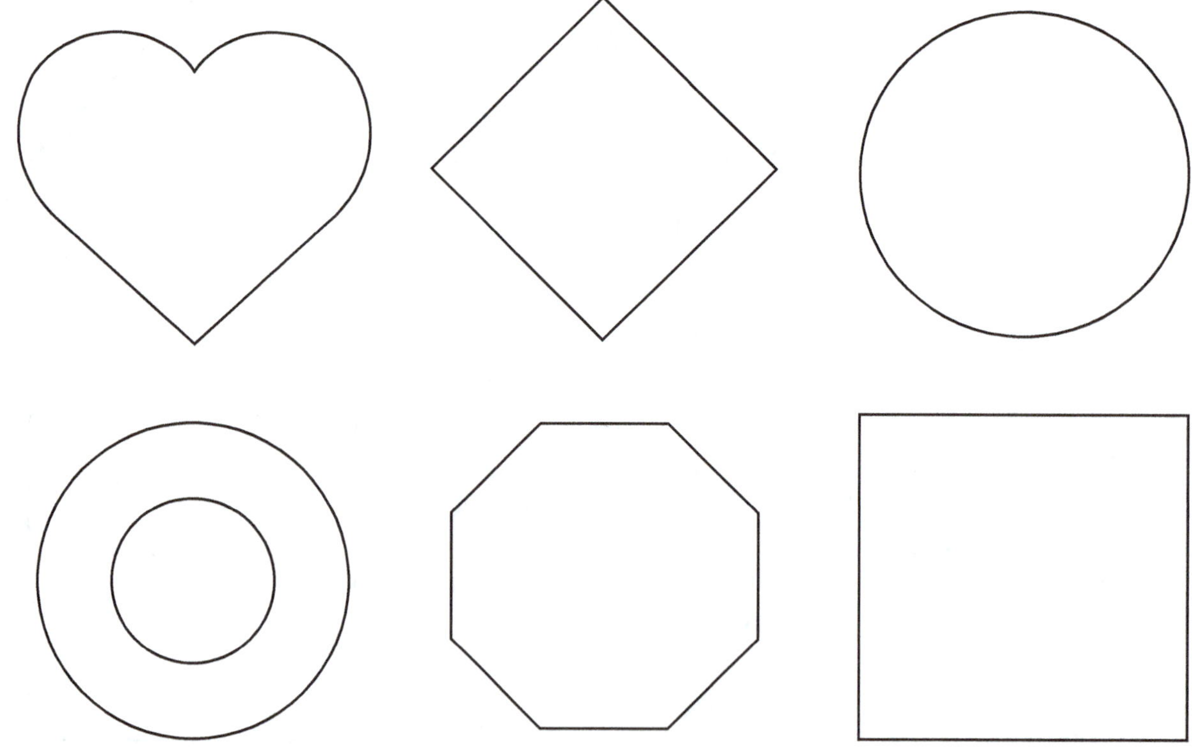

STOP

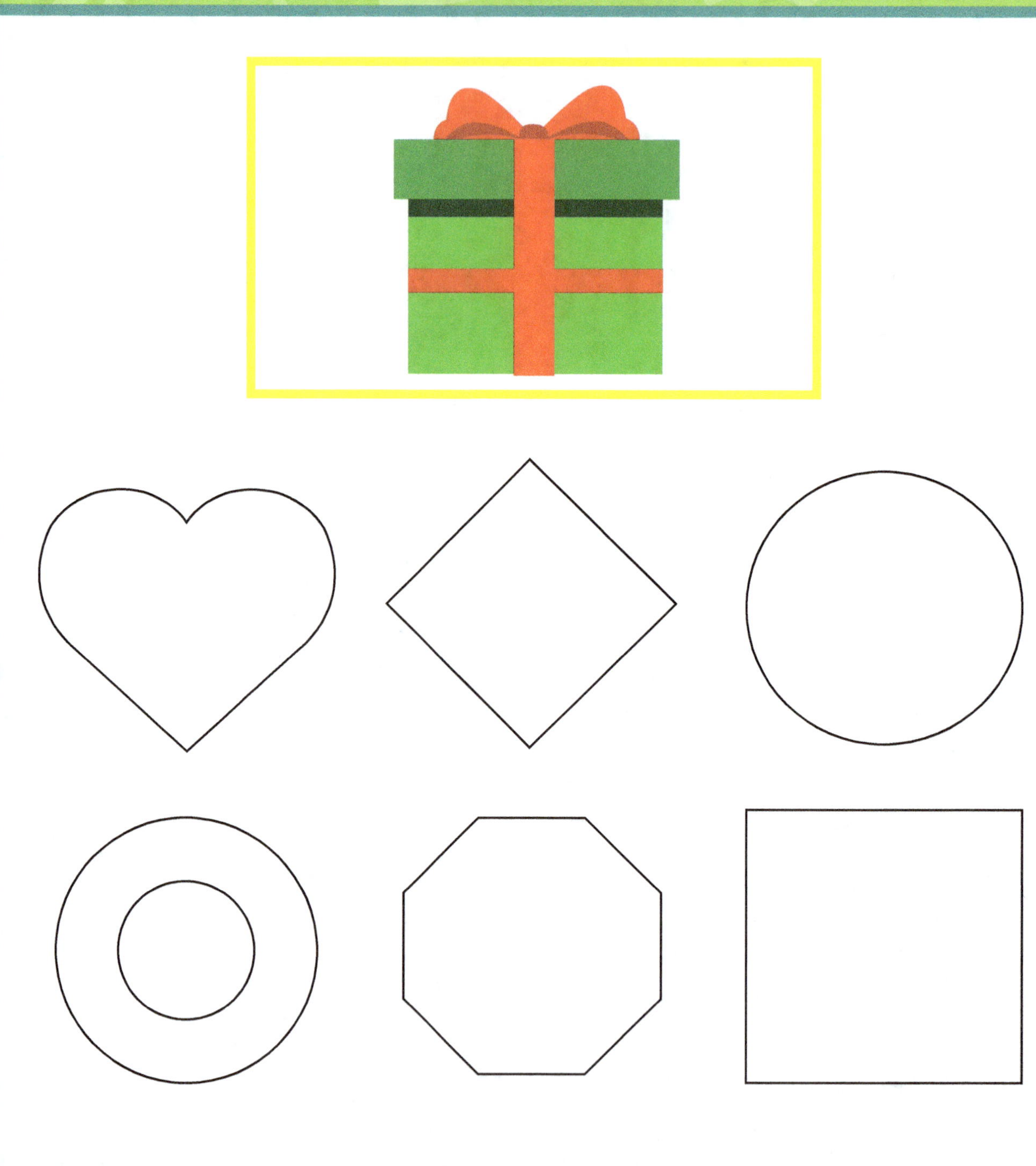

ANSWERS!

EXERCISE NO. 1
HEXAGON
CIRCLE
SQUARE
TRIANGLE

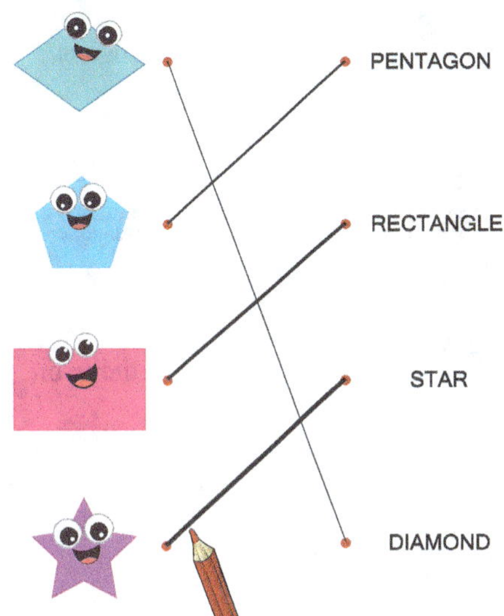

EXERCISE NO. 2
PENTAGON
RECTANGLE
STAR
DIAMOND

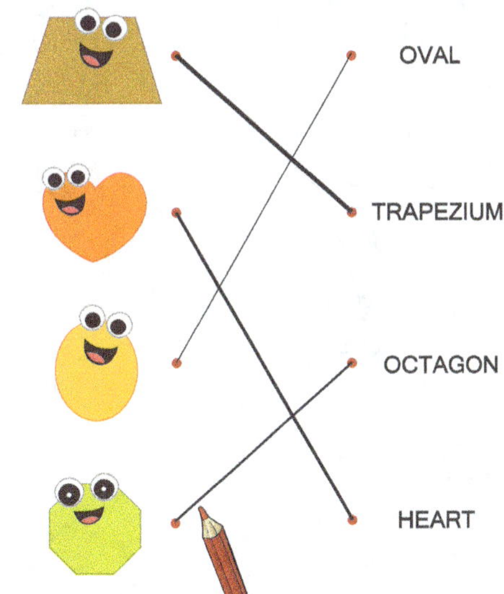

EXERCISE NO. 3
OVAL
TRAPEZIUM
OCTAGON
HEART

EXERCISE NO. 4

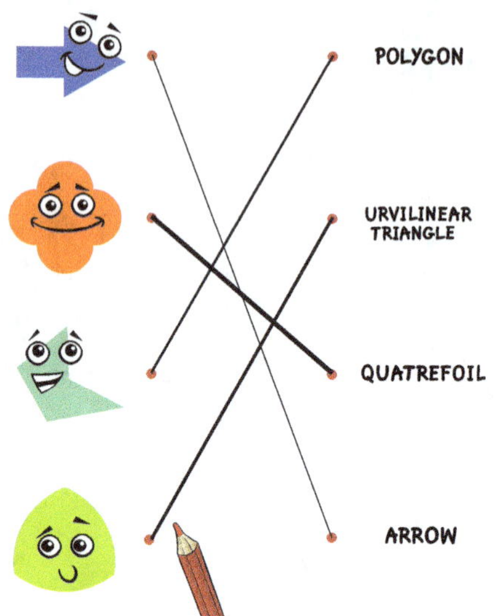

EXERCISE NO. 5

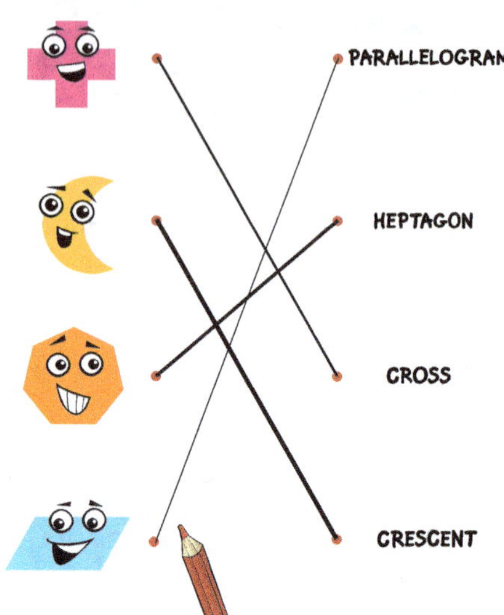

EXERCISE NO. 6

- Color the squares

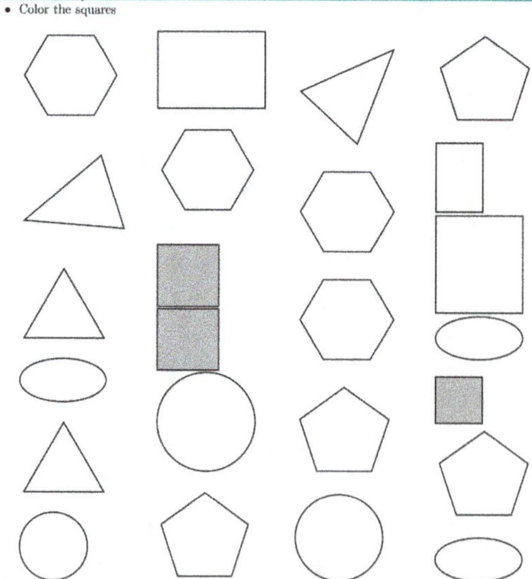

EXERCISE NO. 7

- Color the rectangles

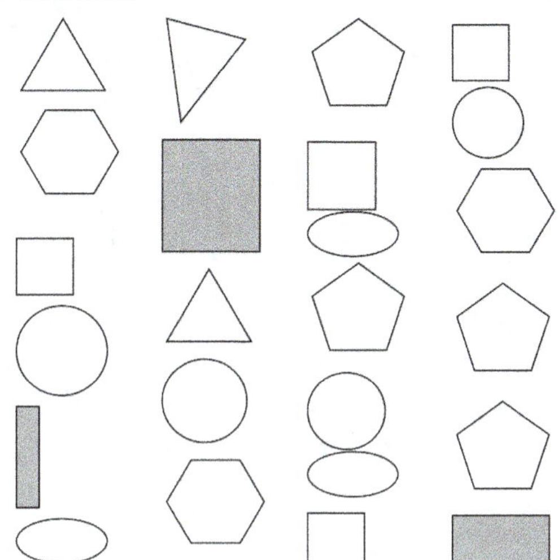

EXERCISE NO. 8

- Color the triangles

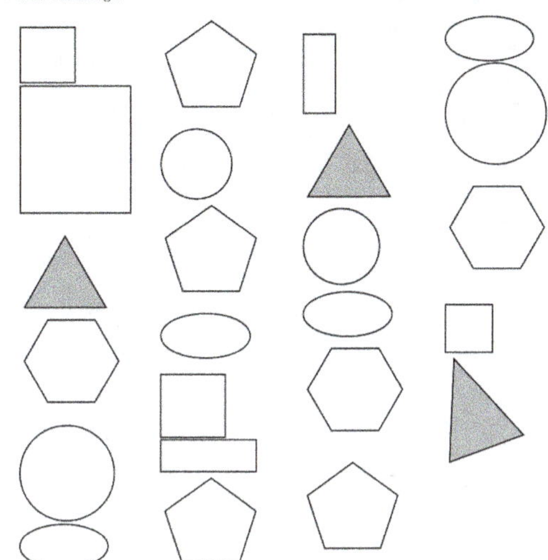

EXERCISE NO. 9

- Color the circles

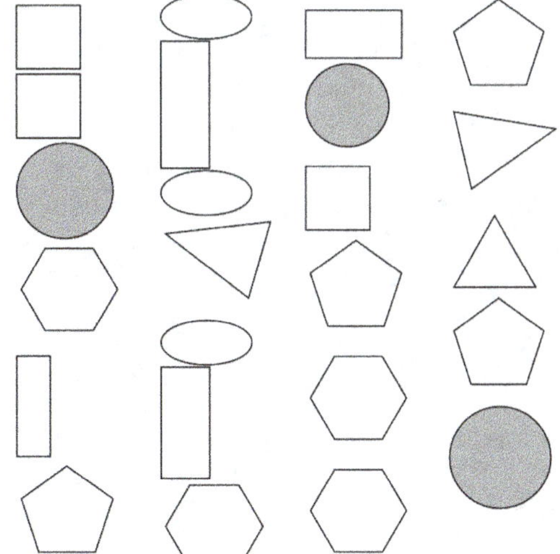

EXERCISE NO. 10

- Color the ovals

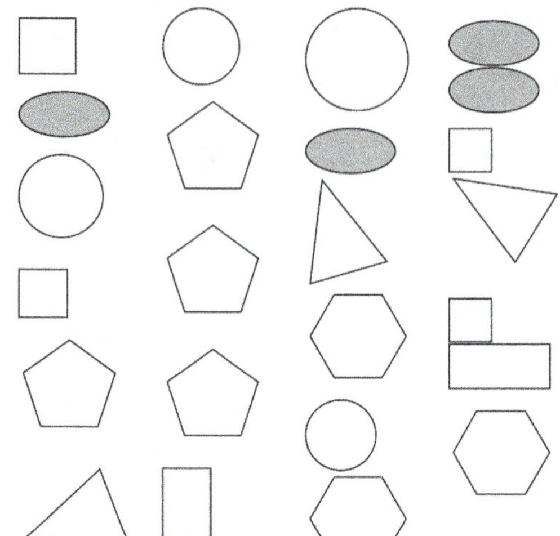

EXERCISE NO. 11

- Color the pentagons

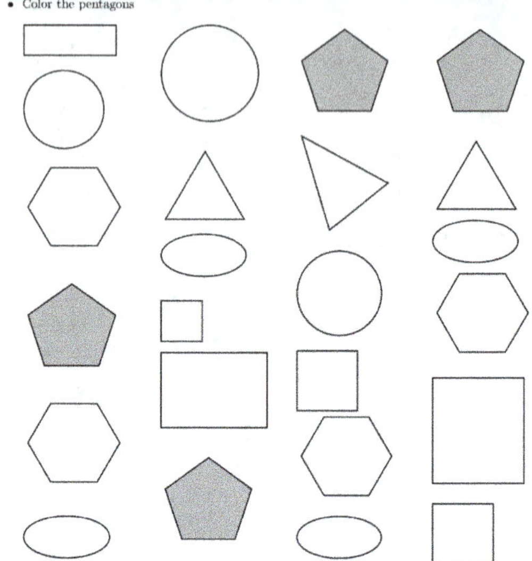

EXERCISE NO. 12

- Color the hexagons

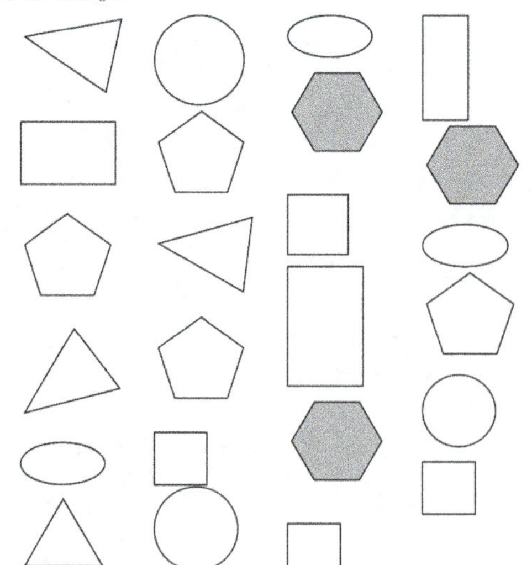

EXERCISE NO. 13

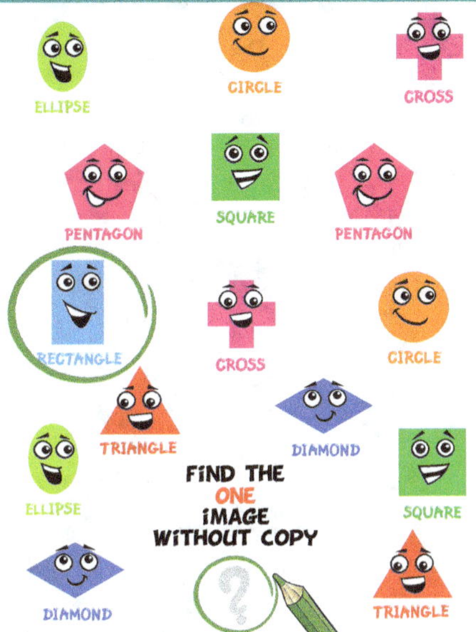

EXERCISE NO. 14

EXERCISE NO. 15

EXERCISE NO. 16

EXERCISE NO. 17

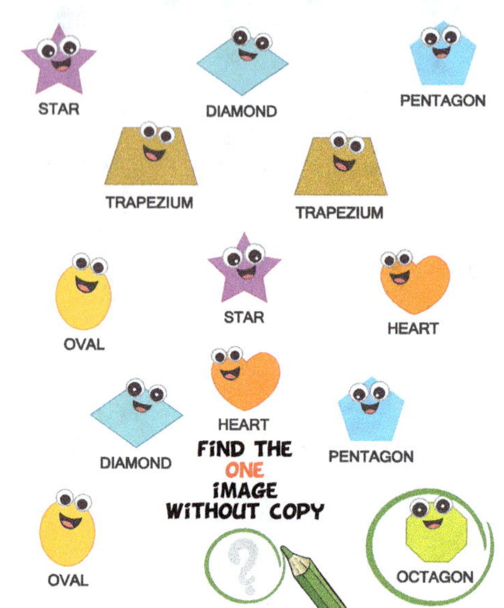

EXERCISE NO. 18

EXERCISE NO. 19

EXERCISE NO. 20

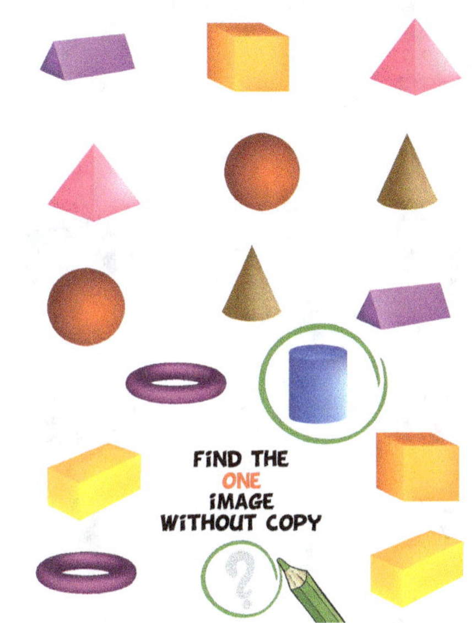

EXERCISE NO. 21

EXERCISE NO. 22

EXERCISE NO. 23

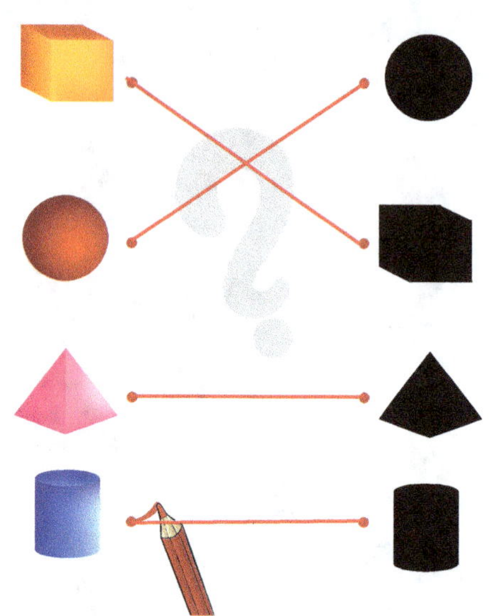

EXERCISE NO. 24

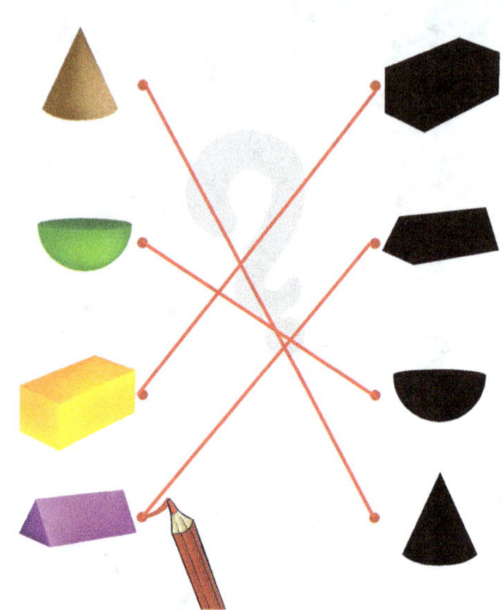

EXERCISE NO. 25

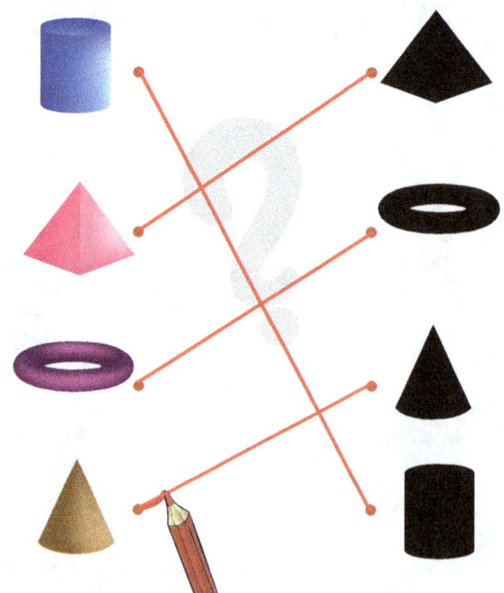

EXERCISE NO. 26

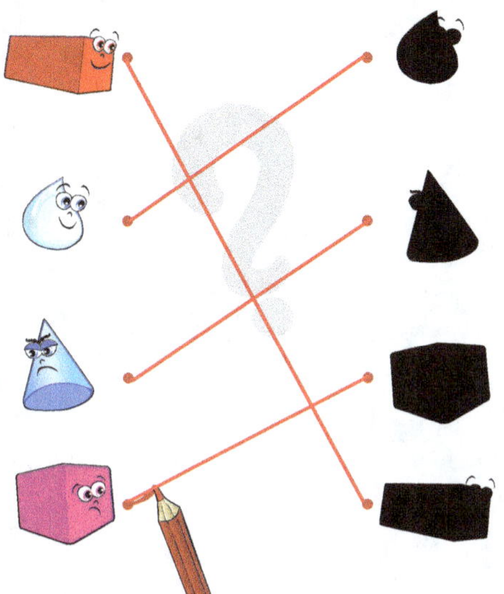

EXERCISE NO. 27

EXERCISE NO. 28

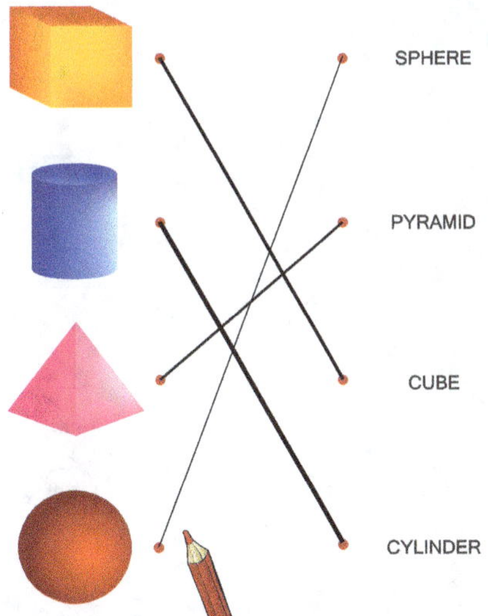

EXERCISE NO. 29

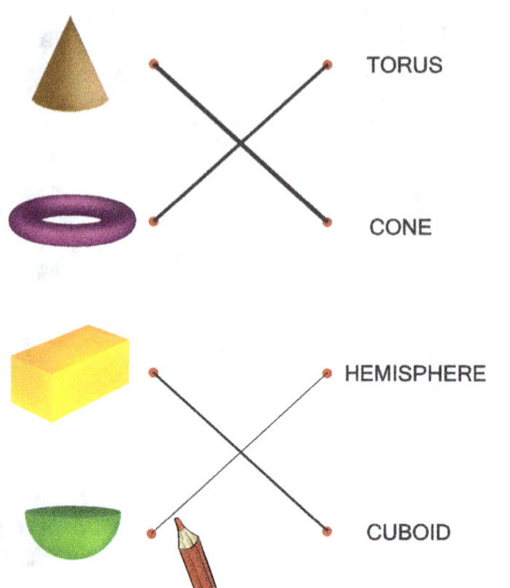
TORUS
CONE
HEMISPHERE
CUBOID

EXERCISE NO. 30

EXERCISE NO. 31

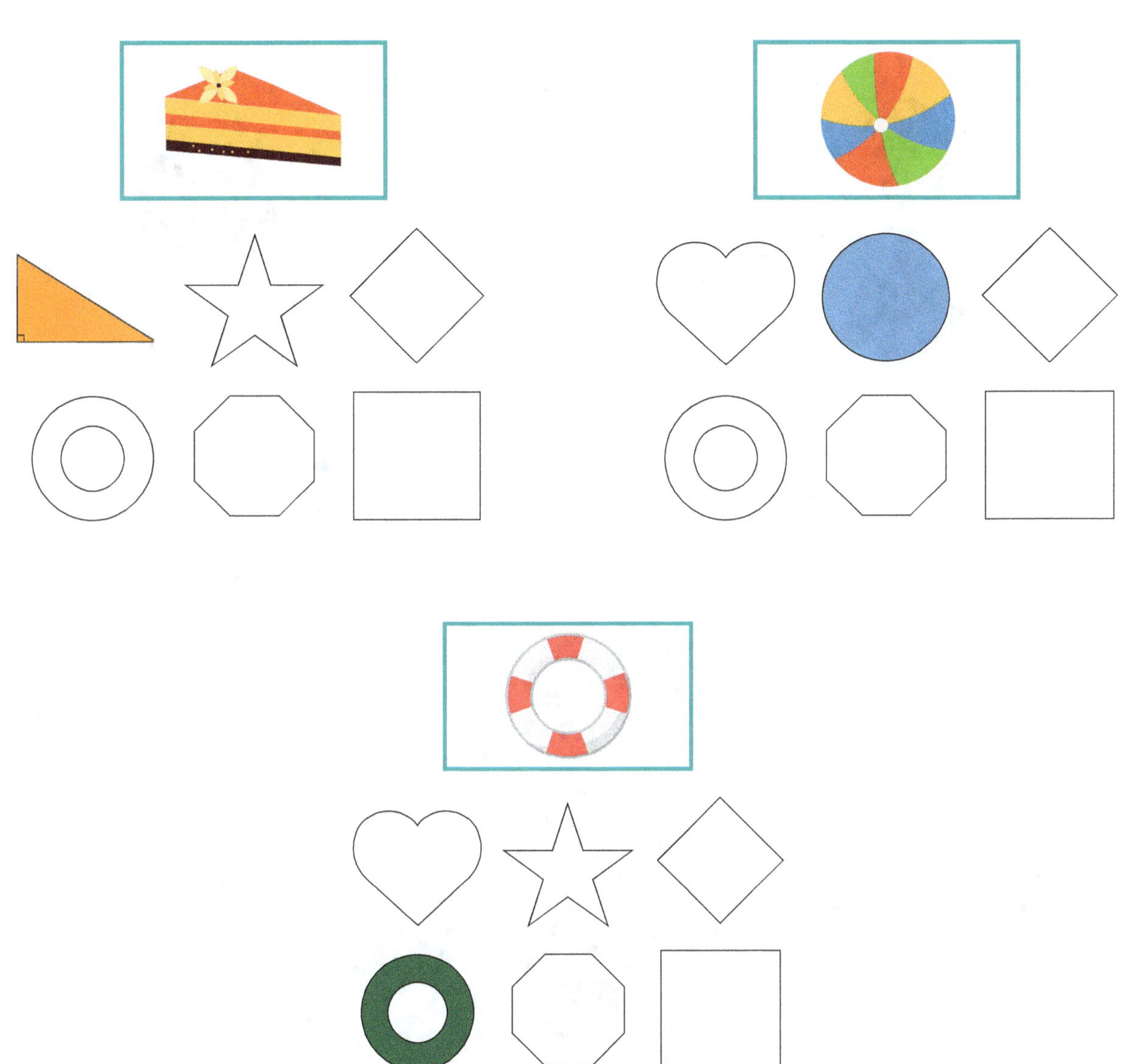

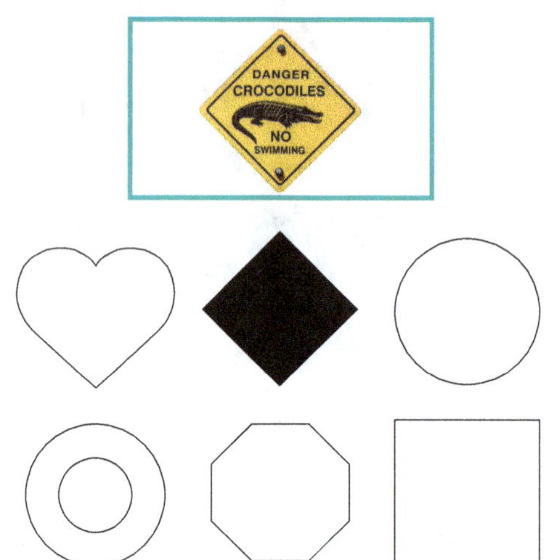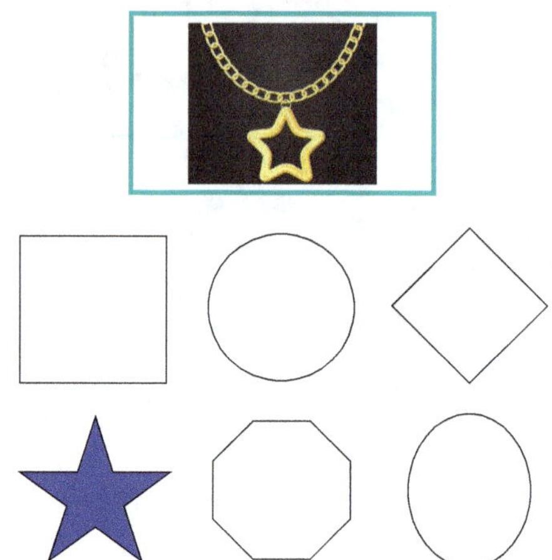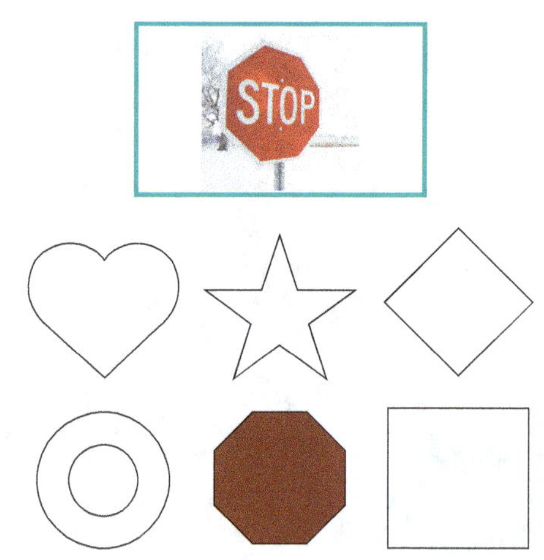

Visit

BABY PROFESSOR
EDUCATION KIDS

www.BabyProfessorBooks.com
to download Free Baby Professor eBooks
and view our catalog of new and exciting
Children's Books